Brand new hilarious jokes

Dad Jokes

The Funniest Yet

hamlyn

First published in Great Britain in
2024 by Hamlyn, an imprint of
Octopus Publishing Group Ltd
Carmelite House
50 Victoria Embankment
London EC4Y 0DZ
www.octopusbooks.co.uk

An Hachette UK Company
www.hachette.co.uk

Text Copyright © Kit Chilvers 2024
Design and layout copyright
© Octopus Publishing Group
Ltd 2024

Distributed in the US by Hachette
Book Group
1290 Avenue of the Americas
4th and 5th Floors, New York,
NY 10104

Distributed in Canada by Canadian
Manda Group
664 Annette St., Toronto,
Ontario, Canada M6S 2C8

ISBN 978-1-783-25548-1

A CIP catalogue record for this
book is available from the British
Library.

Printed and bound in the UK

10 9 8 7 6 5 4 3

Commissioning Editor:
Louisa Johnson
Senior Editor: Pauline Bache
Editorial Assistant: Constance Lam
Designer: The Oak Studio
Creative Director: Mel Four
Senior Production Manager:
Katherine Hockley

This FSC® label means that
materials used for this product
have been responsibly sourced.

MIX
Paper | Supporting
responsible forestry
FSC® C104740
FSC
www.fsc.org

Brand new hilarious jokes

Dad Jokes

The Funniest Yet

@DadSaysJokes

hamlyn

Dedicated to Iyrah Williams – one
half of the dynamic duo
behind Pubity Group and the
@DadSaysJokes brand alongside
Kit. Keep the good times coming.

Introduction

Greetings, fellow jokesters and welcome to another chortle-fest courtesy of @DadSaysJokes! If you've stumbled upon this book in search of enlightenment, humour or perhaps just a way to torment your loved ones with puns aplenty, then you're in for a treat. Welcome to a treasure trove of wit, whimsy and shameless punnery.

A word of caution – with great dad jokes comes great responsibility. Remember that not every audience will appreciate your comedic genius. Just watch the eyes roll, it's all part of the fun – or should I say, pun.

As always, thanks to our huge and ever-growing community on Facebook, Instagram, Threads and X (Twitter) for the witty banter and savagely funny comments on our social pages. They're often funnier than the original jokes. Keep it all coming!

Lots of love as always,
Kit and Andrew

I had a brief relationship with someone who worked at a camera factory.

It never developed.

_____

Pinocchio hasn't had much luck on dating apps.

But what do you expect from a guy who's looking for a relationship with no strings attached?

I used to be really into Egyptian architecture until I realized it was just a giant pyramid scheme.

What do skunks say at church?

Let us spray...

My partner is sleeping in the spare bedroom because she said she has had enough of my night-time Elvis impersonations.

I knocked on her door at 3am and said, "Are You Lonesome Tonight?"

———

What building in New York City has the most stories?

The Public Library.

Do you know what a wok is?

A wok is what you throw at a wabbit when you don't have a wifle.

———

I replaced my rooster with a duck.

Now I wake up at the quack of dawn.

I accidentally dropped a bucket of paint on my boss at the job site.

Boy was he blue in the face!

———

What's the name of the man who is always well prepared for anything?

Justin Case.

Do you know why ironing pants makes them smaller?

Because it de-creases them.

———————

What's the most expensive lamb dish?

Lamb-borghini.

Why did the man sell yeast?

To raise some dough.

My friend dropped his Italian pastries on the floor.

What he's going through I cannelloni imagine.

It was so cold yesterday my computer froze...

It was my own fault though, I left too many windows open.

What happens when a man in Prague tries to buy a trampoline?

The Czech bounces.

What did the full glass say to the empty glass?

Go home. You look drunk.

What's the most popular car in Norway?

The Fjord Explorer.

What is the sleepiest fruit?

The napricot!

If there's a king-sized mattress and a queen-sized mattress, where does the prince sleep?

The heir mattress.

The ice company lost power at their warehouse.

They had to liquidate their entire inventory.

Why did the dog get arrested?

He had unpaid barking tickets.

I recently took a pole and found out that 99 per cent of people in the tent were angry when it collapsed.

I was in line at the bank when a man got pulled from the queue and escorted out by security, just for having flames tattooed around his biceps.

Apparently they don't allow fire arms in the building.

———————

There's a lot to consider before getting married. On the one hand, you get to wear a ring. On the other, you don't.

I found $20 lying in the parking lot and thought to myself "What would Jesus do?"

So, I turned it into wine.

———

Five-quarters of people won't admit...

That they're bad with fractions.

Me: I've been tired for five years.

My kid: That's how old I am.

Me: Oh, weird.

What part of "I don't want to spend any more money" don't I understand?

My brother used to beat me up every morning as a kid.

He would get up at 6:55am, I would wake up at 7.

I got a joke about pizza but it's too cheesy.

What do astronauts put on their toast?

Space jam!

I dreamed last night that my spirit rose from a toilet bowl.

It was an out-of-potty experience.

Dr Victor Frankenstein entered a bodybuilding contest.

Upon arrival, he realized he misunderstood the objective.

Two clowns are eating a cannibal.

One turns to the other and says, "I think we got this joke wrong."

Just found out the company that produces yardsticks won't be making them any longer.

What do you call it when a king passes gas?

Air to the throne.

I taught my pet wolf how to meditate.

Now he's aware wolf.

Every morning after I wake up, the first thing I do is make my bed.

Tomorrow I'm returning this piece of junk to IKEA.

What do flowers study in high school?

STEM.

I don't wanna party like it's 1999.
I wanna go grocery shopping like
it's 1999.

Every morning, I take my cow on a long walk through the local vineyard.

I herd it through the grapevine.

———

PSA to the dads out there: when your kid says, "I want Mummy," what they are really saying is, "I'd like to speak to your supervisor, please."

My fortune cookie doesn't have my message inside.

How unfortunate.

Who did Noah hire to design his boat?

An arkitect.

Brought my own spoon to my cooking class last night.

It caused quite a stir.

Got stuck for ages behind Satan in the queue at the Post Office. For the devil takes many forms.

In a safety meeting at work they asked me what steps I'd take in a fire.

Apparently "Really big and fast ones" was the wrong answer.

———————

A man is staying in a hotel. He walks up to the front desk and says, "Sorry, I forgot what room I'm in, can you help me?"

The receptionist replies, "No problem, sir. This is the lobby."

Gave a presentation about wind energy yesterday.

It was a breeze.

Why is the mathematics book sad?

It has too many problems.

What do you call a cow that's just given birth?

Decalfinated.

_____

What's the opposite of irony?

Wrinkly.

Just learned that EOD does NOT mean "end of December" and now I have quite a bit of explaining to do.

A robber broke into a college bookstore and stole $23,000 worth of textbooks.

Fortunately, the police were able to return both books to the school.

Why did the Italian chef stop preparing dinner?

He ran out of thyme.

I don't know how many coffees it takes to be friendly, but so far it's not 12.

Just found out there's a new type of broom and it's sweeping the nation.

What do you call the fear of Santa?

Claustrophobia.

I think somebody was cutting wood around here.

I saw dust.

I passed all my courses except for Greek mythology.

That has always been my Achilles' elbow.

I knew a guy who was arrested for stealing hay.

Unfortunately, he couldn't make bale.

The excessively loud jeweller made my earring.

A sweater I bought was picking up static electricity so I returned it to the store.

They gave me another one free of charge.

———————

I once knew a guy who injured himself on the toilet.

Good thing it was only a minor flush wound.

What do you call a restaurant that sells only beans?

A gas station.

_____

What do you call a person that takes care of owls?

A hootin' nanny!

Just fired myself from cleaning my house. I don't like my attitude and I got caught drinking on the job.

————————

Went to a restaurant run by kleptomaniacs.

The waiter took my order.

What do you call two guys who love maths?

Algebros.

Cattle farmers are technically always raising the steaks.

What was the snowman doing in the vegetable patch?

Picking his nose.

I was at a party when a monster rolled his eyes at me.

So I rolled them back to him.

Got fired from the clock factory.

All I did was put in some extra hours!

How are dad jokes like a good pair of running shoes?

They're good for the sole.

Just got a new job at the broth factory.

Came with great stock options.

Why did the police arrest the turkey?

Because they suspected fowl play.

_____

Just received a mind-controlled
calculator for my birthday.

Not the greatest present but it's the
thought that counts.

Did you hear about the big fight at the seafood restaurant?

Battered fish everywhere.

What does Jeff Bezos do every night before bed?

He puts his pajamazon.

If you are ambushed at night, then technically you have been pmbushed.

I usually don't joke about drinking straight liquor.

But I guess I'll give it a shot.

I just ate a frozen apple.

Hardcore.

———

Why couldn't the pirate call his mum?

She left the phone off the hook.

My friend Pete
believes he was
reincarnated from a
previous life.

We call him Repete.

If you ever need me, I'm always just five missed calls, four text messages and three voicemails away.

Why did the snowman get detention?

He was up to snow good.

To the man who stole my identity...

Who the hell do you think you are?

Why don't escaped convicts make good authors?

Because they never finish their sentences.

Scientists recently managed to weigh a rainbow.

Turns out it was pretty light.

———

What did the pirate get on his report card?

Seven Cs.

My doctor advised me to cut down on my sodium intake.

I took her advice with a pinch of salt.

———

My partner is mad at the fact that I have no sense of direction.

So I packed up my stuff and right.

I asked my partner if I was the only one they had ever been with.

They said, "Yes, all the others were all nines and tens."

What do you get when you divide the circumference of a jack o'lantern by its diameter?

Pumpkin pi.

Not all Excel puns are terrible.

Just SUM.

––––––––––––

Why did the tree go to the hairdresser?
Its roots were showing.

I have been
teaching my dog
to fetch tools from
my workshop.
He's not perfect.

But he knows
the drill.

What happens if the average number of bullies at a school goes up?

The mean increases.

_____

I've always been hesitant to post Monopoly puns but today I thought I'd take a Chance.

When a woman says "What?", it is not because she didn't hear you. She is actually giving you a second chance to change what you said.

———

How do you make a tissue dance?

Put a little boogie in it.

All those years of boarding school and I still don't know the proper way to enter a plane.

Why did the house go to the doctor?

It was having window panes.

Cannibals will never go hungry.

They can always make themselves
a snack.

———————

I have a condition where I can't stop
telling airport jokes.

My doctor says it's terminal.

I'm the type of dad who helps my kids look for their chocolate bar that I ate.

When I came home from work, my partner said, "Ugh, the baby has been crying for hours. Can you take over?"

I said, "Sure," and started crying for hours.

What do you use to open a haunted house?

A spoo-key.

Did you hear about the opera singer who threw the game opening baseball?

They say she had perfect pitch.

I'm currently reading a book about a couple of insects who fall in love in an Italian city.

It's a Rome ants novel.

What did the pirate say on his 80th birthday?

Aye matey!

How do you know when a man is about to say something smart?

When he starts his sentence with, "A woman once told me…"

The struggle bus should have a loyalty rewards programme.

How do you stop a bull from charging?

Take away its credit card.

I made a movie about a glass jug.

It was nominated for Best Pitcher.

Why did the bank robbers call their travel agent?

To plan a getaway.

_____

A boy went to the doctor with broccoli in his ears and sweets up his nose.

The doctor told him that he wasn't eating right.

I've never owned a real pair of binoculars before.

But it's something I'd like to look into.

Just opened three birthday cards and I'm up £150!

I love being a postman.

Why did the Tooth Fairy go to jail?

She was guilty of incisor trading.

———

So Fred Flintstone barged in, shouted, "YABBADAB—," then left without further ado.

I caught my neighbour stealing my socks off my clothesline.

I was going to confront him, but I got cold feet.

Unfortunately I was misled. I put a bet on a horse that had excellent breeding.

After the horse left the starting gate, he stopped and closed it behind him.

I had a Nirvana joke but I forgot it.

Oh well, whatever...never mind.

———

When's the worst time to have a heart attack?

During a game of charades.

If you were born in September, it's pretty safe to assume that your parents started the new year with a bang.

I'm trying to find a place to sleep after my partner kicked me out of bed...

Sofa, so good.

Why was everyone so tired on April 1st?

Because they just finished a long 31-day March.

What do you call a number that can't stay in place?

A roamin numeral.

I recently ordered a new sail for my boat. A few days later I realized I'd made a mistake and called to change the order.

The person who answered said, "Sorry, that sail has shipped!"

Me: Dad, are you going to eat dinner with your friend Jeff?

Dad: No, he's out of town.

Me: I meant your other friend Jeff.

Dad: He isn't in town either…we're Jeff-free.

Marriage is like going to a restaurant. You order what you want, then when you see what someone else has, you wish you had ordered that.

How do you hire a horse?

Put up a ladder.

My manager told me to have a good day. So I didn't go into work.

What do kids play when they have nothing else to do?

Bored games.

What did the boy say to his fingers?

I'm counting on you.

What kind of music do elves listen to?

Wrap music.

What do cake and baseball have in common?

They both need a batter.

———————

When does Friday come before Thursday?

In the dictionary.

Today at the gym I asked a hot person what their New Year's resolution was.

They said: "Screw you!"

So I'm pretty excited for the new year!

What did the tree say when spring finally arrived?

What a re-leaf.

How can you tell if a pig is hot?

It's bacon.

Did you hear about the guy who was afraid of hurdles?

He got over it.

Why did the drum go to bed?

It was beat.

_____

What do you call a rude cow?

Beef jerky.

Did you hear about the guy who drank invisible ink? He's at the hospital waiting to be seen.

How do mice floss their teeth?

With string cheese.

————

I hope my partner is OK. He's barely touched the 184 birds I gave him over the 12 days of Christmas.

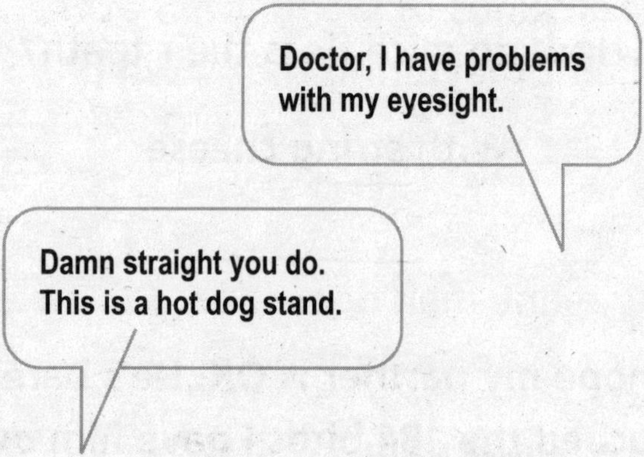
Doctor, I have problems with my eyesight.
Damn straight you do. This is a hot dog stand.

I get all kinds of weird looks at the gym.
Can't they bring their own pizza?

How many men does it take to screw in
a light bulb?

One. He just holds it up there and waits
for the world to revolve around him.

What do dentists call their X-rays?

Tooth pics!

Why did the melon jump into the lake?

It wanted to be a watermelon.

Grandma: Back in our day, you could get bread, milk, soaps, spices, eggs, meat, all for a dollar.

Grandchild: You can't do that now. They have CCTV everywhere!

Why won't it hurt if you hit your friend with a 2-litre bottle of soda?

Because it's a soft drink!

What has four wheels and flies?

A garbage truck.

What happens if a seagull flies over the bay?

It will become a bagel!

What music do planets like to listen to?

Neptunes.

What lights up a stadium?

A match.

Why does God only let 5 per cent of people into heaven?

Because if God let any more in, it would be hell.

Why do cemeteries have gates?

Because people are dying to get in.

How did the barber win the race?

He took a shortcut.

Why do they not play poker in the jungle?

There are too many cheetahs.

What is the easiest way to burn
1,000 calories?

Leave the pizza in the oven.

Why are pirates called pirates?

Because they arrrr!

What do you call a cold dog?

A chilli dog!

———————

What is the best way to get a man to stop chewing on his nails?

Make him keep his shoes on.

Did you hear about the cat that ate a lemon?

Now it's a sour puss.

I had a construction joke to crack.

But I can't tell it now as it is still a "work in progress".

What is a fake spaghetti called?

An im-pasta.

My partner told me they want to spice up our love life.

So I bought them a chilli pepper.

What runs around
the yard but
doesn't move?

A fence.

Why did the dinosaur cross the road?

Because chickens weren't evolved then.

What did the frog order at the café?

French flies.

Which key opens a banana? Monkey.

How do you make an apple upside-down cake?

Push it down the hill.

Why was the torch happy?

It was lit.

What gets more wet the more it dries?

A towel!

Why did the banana go to the doctor?

Because it did not peel well.

What did one ocean say to the other ocean?

Nothing, they just waved.

What do pampered cows produce?

Spoiled milk.

I told my doctor that I had broken my arm in two places.

She told me to stop going to those places.

What do you call an alligator in a vest?

An investigator.

_____

How do you fix a broken tomato?

Tomato paste.

A maths teacher had four apples in one hand and five in the other. What did she have altogether?

Two big hands.

What kind of water doesn't freeze?

Hot water.

What do you call a sleeping dinosaur?

Dino snore.

Why did the cat run away from the tree?

Its bark scared him!

How come teddy bears never want to eat anything?

Because they're always stuffed.

_____

What's a plant's favourite drink?

Root beer!

A magician was driving down the road and turned into a driveway.

A horse walks into a bar.

The bartender says, "Why the long face?"

Why didn't the bullet come to work today?

Because he got fired.

_____

Which is Minnie Mouse's favourite car?

A Minnie van.

In a race, how did one tomato cheer the other?

Ketchup!

_____

The duck bought lip gloss and said what?

Put it on my bill.

What has two legs but can't walk?

A pair of trousers.

Why did the boy throw a piece of butter out the window?

He wanted to see a butterfly.

What did "0" say to "8"?

Nice belt.

Why do giraffes have long necks?

Because they have smelly feet.

———

**What would you do if an elephant sat
on your fence?**

Get a new fence.

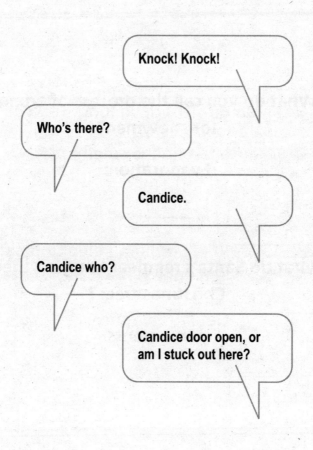

What do you call the process of aging for snowmen?

Evaporation.

_____

What do Santa's reindeer hang on their Christmas trees?

Hornaments.

Where do pirates go when they are sick?

They go to the dock!

How many lips does a flower have?

Tu-lips!

Do you know what you will get if you ever cross a vampire with a snowman?

Frostbite.

What do you have when both your son and daughter text you to lend them £100 each?

You have £200 and two unread messages on your phone!

———

My wife texted saying that she was having a terribly stressful day at work and was losing her entire mind.

I texted back, "Relax. It's all in your head."

What's a skeleton's favourite instrument?

A trom-bone!

How do you cook an alligator?

With a croc-pot.

I lost my shoes at the party. I think it is a fairy tale.

No, it’s because you were drunk.

How does a squid prepare itself for battle?

It goes to a battle well armed!

———————

Two peanuts were walking in the town.
But one was a-salted.

Name a dog that can do magic.

Labracadabrador!

_____

A and C were going to prank their
friend...but they just letter B.

What's the biggest difference between Thanksgiving and April Fools' Day?

On one, you're thankful, but on the other, you're prankful.

I went to school for magicians but failed
the final exam. They were all
trick questions.

———————

Without doubt, my favourite Robin
Williams movie is "Mrs Fire."

Why is the obtuse triangle always frustrated?

It is never right.

_____

What do you call ticks in space?

Luna-ticks.

Did you hear about the man who won the gold medal at the Olympics?

He had it bronzed.

_____

I told my computer I needed a break, and now it won't stop sending me vacation ads.

I only know three jokes. One about construction, another about pizza and a third about philosophy. But don't worry, they're all up for interpretation.

Why was the equal sign so humble?

Because it knew it wasn't less than or greater than anyone else.

————

I only tell dad jokes on days that end in "y".

Who needs a day for the fools when you're surrounded by them all year?

———

Why did the programmer quit his job?

He didn't get arrays.

Why did the woman bring a ladder to the bar?

Because she heard the drinks were on the house!

———

My partner told me I should be more spontaneous.

So I bought a zoo.

I asked my wife if she ever googles her ex.

She said, "Not since the judge ordered me to stop."

My partner told me they want a man who can make them laugh.

So I showed them my bank statement.

I asked my friend if they ever talk to themselves.

They said, "Only when I need expert advice."

My dad constantly criticizes me for not wearing our traditional Scottish family attire.

He's giving me quite a kilt trip.

Why did the mathematician become a musician?

She had good "algorhythm".

Five ants rented an apartment with another five ants. Now they're tenants.

My wife told me to take the spider out instead of killing him. Went out. Had a few drinks. Nice guy. He's a web designer.

I asked my husband if he believes in love at first sight.

He said, "Of course, that's why I stopped looking."

———————

What did the biologist wear to impress his date?

Designer genes.

Waiter: How do you like your steak, sir?

Diner: Like winning an argument with my partner.

Waiter: Rare it is.

Why did the physics teacher break up with the history teacher?

They couldn't agree on the fundamental principles.

Just got hospitalized due to a peekaboo accident. They put me in the ICU.

The Indian restaurant I work for is so secretive I had to sign a legal agreement that I wouldn't share the flatbread recipe. Just their standard naan disclosure agreement.

My partner asked me if I could stop singing "Wonderwall". I said maybe.

I've decided I want a pet termite. I'm going to call him Clint. Clint Eatswood.

Why haven't aliens visited our solar system yet?

They looked at the reviews...
Only one star.

I am giving up drinking for a month.

Sorry that came out wrong.

I am giving up. Drinking for a month.

I accidentally took my cat's meds last night...Don't ask meow.

Why did the man bring a suitcase to the kitchen?

Because he wanted to pack a lunch.

_____

After getting on well chatting online, I was late for my date with an electrician...

By the time I got there, the spark had gone.

What do you call imaginary people from Sweden?

Artificial Swedeners.

Today I plan on being as useless as the "g" in lasagna.

My partner looked up at me with tears streaming down their face and said, "I can't do this anymore."

So I took over chopping up the onions.

So when I was in a shoe shop this morning trying on a pair, I said to the assistant, "It's too tight."

They said, "Try it with the tongue out."

I said, "It'th nho ghood, it'th thill thoo thight."

———

Why did the person bring a pencil to bed?

In case they wanted to draw the curtains!

Politicians and diapers have one thing in common. They should both be changed regularly, and for the same reason.

How is it one careless match can start a forest fire, but it takes a whole box to start a campfire?

For those who don't want Alexa listening in on their conversations... They're making a male version...it doesn't listen to anything.

———————

Apparently exercising helps with decision making. It's true! I went for a jog today and decided I'm never going again.

My son likes to cause a scene by going up to his loft and playing the bongos very loudly. It's a little drum attic.

What do you call a snake that works for the government?

A civil serpent!

———————

I made a chicken salad yesterday...
Turns out they prefer grain.

So apparently "to leave" wasn't an appropriate answer when my manager asked, "What are your goals this year?"

What did the whale say after eating a ship?

"I can't believe I ate the hull thing."

When my wife was in labour, I would tell her jokes to distract her from the pain, but she didn't seem amused. It must have been the delivery.

The guy who stole my diary and Bible got in a serious car accident. My thoughts and prayers are with him.

If you ever open your own business, try selling stoves. You'll offer a range of hot products.

Why did the newspaper blush?

It saw the comic strip!

I heard a joke about chocolate bars.
It wasn't very funny. But I still Snickered.

People are so excited for the new
aquarium to open, they've camped
out for days and have dressed up as
dolphins, narwhals and whales.

The aquarium just announced no
admission fee for these dedicated
visitors. So for all in tents and
porpoises, it's free.

The lizard store is struggling to remain open. It's had financial issues right from the gecko.

Is it OK that I start drinking as soon as the kids get to school? Or does that make me a bad teacher?

————————

Never tell secrets in a garden.
The potatoes have eyes, the corn has ears and the beans talk.

You thought that aquatic explosive puns are bad? Just wait until you sea mine.

What did the dentist say when his girlfriend broke up with him?

I'm flossed without you!

When your partner starts a sentence with "When you get a chance..." just go ahead and start putting your shoes on. They mean now.

What did one pig say to the other on Valentine's Day?

Don't go bacon my heart.

My half-brother and I aren't allowed to play with chainsaws anymore.

Are you a bank loan? Because you got my interest.

———————

What did the painter tell his girlfriend?

"I love you with all my art."

What do snakes do after they fight?
They hiss and make up.

What type of undergarments does a lawyer wear?

Legal briefs.

My mother asked me to hand out invites for my brother's surprise birthday party.

That's when I realized he was the favourite twin.

———

What do you call a baby monkey?

A chimp off the old block.

My favourite band just released a Christmas song called, "Duvet Know It's Christmas?"

It's a cover song.

How do you send a message in the forest?

By moss code.

I've decided to open a small newsstand that will also sell frozen yogurt. I'm calling it "Froyo Information".

What do you call a country that doesn't exist?

A halluci-nation!

_____

What do cows tell each other at bedtime?

Dairy tales!

The bad news is, I accidentally took the wrong medication today. The good news is, I'm now protected from heartworms and fleas for the next three months.

Whoever said "out of sight, out of mind" never had a spider disappear in the bedroom.

———————

Did you know that bowling alleys are so quiet...you can hear a pin drop.

What is a horse's favourite kind of pasta?

Pen-neigh!

Why couldn't the lifeguard save the hippie?

He was too far out, man.

———————

If at first you don't drink tea...
Chai again.

Need an ark? I Noah guy.

Scientists have found that cows produce more milk when the farmer talks to them. Apparently it's a case of in one ear and out the udder.

Hot dogs don't like to take videos at concerts. They prefer to relish the moment.

———————

Two artists had a fight. It ended in a draw.

My wife asked me to take her to one of those restaurants where they prepare the food right in front of you. So I took her to Subway and that's how the fight began.

———————

While doing his history homework, my son asked me what I knew about Galileo. I said, "he's just a poor boy from a poor family."

My extra-sensitive toothpaste doesn't like it when I use other toothpastes.

What's the difference between a knight and Santa's reindeer?

The knight is slayin' the dragon, and the reindeer are draggin' the sleigh.

Told my partner our next-door neighbour died.

They said, "Who? Ray?"

I told them it was way too early to celebrate like that.

———————

I'm like four days past my bedtime. 40s may be the new 20s but 9pm is the new midnight.

I was robbed at the gas station today!
I called the police and they asked if
I knew who did it. I said yes, pump
number 6.

———

Just accidentally put my donor card into
the ATM machine. It cost me an arm
and a leg.

Me: Hi, do you take walk-ins?

The funeral director: What?

The clerk asked debit or credit?
I whipped out a twenty and told her to
never again assume my tender.

———————

Making new friends as an adult is hard
because the people I'd get along best
with are the ones who also don't want
to leave their house.

What do you call a cow with two legs?

Lean beef.

———————

You can tell a lot about a woman by her hands. For instance, if they are around your throat, she's probably feeling mad.

What do you call an attractive monster?

Pretty scary.

What's a quarterback's least favourite pastry?

Turnovers!

Back in the day, William Shakespeare was also known as Billy Wobbleskewer to his mates.

———————

Managed to resuscitate a clown the other day. He's now on laugh support.

So what's your idea of a perfect date?

DD/MM/YYYY. I find other formats confusing.

The next time your wife gets angry, drape a towel over her shoulders like a cape and say, "Now you're SUPER ANGRY!"

Maybe she'll laugh.

Maybe you'll die.

I'm reading a book called *There's a Hole in My Bucket!*

By Lee King.

What did the skydiver say when their pack didn't open?

Chute!

My friend just told me that my daughter and my wife look like twins. I said, "Well they were separated at birth."

I miss the old days when the bills didn't have my name on them.

Do I hear a lion in your closet? Narnia business.

Procaffeination
(*noun*)
The tendency to not start your day (or, anything really) until you've had your first cup of coffee.

What do you call a skeleton in a closet?

A hide and seek winner.

———————

It's hard to write a good drinking song.
I never make it past the first few bars.

What do you call a lazy kangaroo?

A pouch potato!

What do you get when you cross a dog with an antenna?

A golden receiver!

_____

I saw my partner using her phone to record herself getting her hair styled.

I think she's planning to watch the highlights later.

What do you call a neighbourhood Lego celebration? A block party.

Accidentally combined "all good" and "no worries" and said "all worries" and it's the most honest thing I've said all year.

You lost your phone and it's on silent? Too bad. If you liked it you shoulda put a ring on it.

At the airport, my friend suggested we disguise ourselves as luggage. I said, "Let's not get carried away."

What do you call a cow that's under the influence?

High steaks.

My grandpa
reached 110
yesterday. That's
the last time I get
in the car with him
driving.

Really love it when the earth travels
all the way around the sun.
Makes my year.

———————

What happened when Mario crashed
his go kart?

He got Toad.

Job interviewer: It says here you went to Harvard University.

Me: Yes, for my cousin's graduation.

Not to brag, but I just got hired as a fitness model.

They used me as the "before" picture.

_____

I never thought I'd be the kind of person who'd wake up early in the morning to exercise, and turns out I was right.

I was in an 80s band called The Disease.
It was better than The Cure.

———————

I still have my late grandmother in my
contacts. We shouldn't have scattered
her ashes on such a windy day.

There was a Roman emperor who received the gift of eternal youth at the age of 19. His name was Constant Teen.

What do you get when you cross an octopus with a hippopotamus?

You get your funding revoked by the ethics committee.

My local pizzeria has just made the world's largest pizza crust. I'd like to see someone top that.

To eat a whole cake would be to commit the sin of gluttony. But to eat a whole pie is OK, as the sin of pi is always zero.

Are oranges orange because orange is orange, or is orange orange because oranges are orange?

What do you call a janitor who is secretly a spy?

A sweeper agent.

I'd share a humourless joke with you. But where's the pun in that?

If horrific means to be horrible, does terrific mean to be terrible?

———————

Lactose intolerance is a dairy serious issue.

How do you row a canoe filled with puppies?

With a doggy paddle!

Why did the programmer fail his vision test?

Because he couldn't C#.

Would I rather be feared or loved?

Umm easy, both. I want people to be afraid of how much they love me.

My kids got me a box of small rocks and sand for my birthday. It's not the best gift I've ever gotten, but I appreciate the sediment.

Just learned that it was a steroid that killed the dinosaurs so nope you'll never see me taking them.

———————

What did the lions and tigers say to their friend James when he came to visit?

Welcome to the jungle, Jim.

My partner got super mad because I take really long showers and our utility bills are huge. We'll be fine, but right now I'm in hot water.

If we remove all laws the crime rate would be 0 per cent.

It's totally impossible to swap the skins of different citrus fruits. Change my rind.

———

Bacon and eggs walk into a bar. The bartender says, "Sorry, we don't serve breakfast."

Did you hear about the comedian who moved in upstairs? It's actually a pretty funny story.

———

What do you get when you drop a piano down a mine shaft?

A flat minor.

Did you know that by replacing your favourite snacks with grapefruit, you can lose up to 90 per cent of what little joy you still have left in your life.

———

Woke up in a cold sweat, terrified that I overslept for work. But quickly realized I was already at work so breathed a sigh of relief.

My roommates are convinced our house is haunted. I've lived here for 283 years and have never noticed anything strange.

Had a terrible nightmare that I was trapped in the pancake factory. I was tossing and turning all night!

I struggle with Roman numerals until I get to 159. Then it just CLIX.

I poured root beer into a square glass. Now I just have beer.

I was going to invest in a funeral home.

But it's a dying industry.

I've learned so much from my mistakes
that I'm thinking of making a few more.

Did you hear about the head of lettuce who left his job at the church to become a baseball referee?

He is now known as the Holy Romaine Umpire.

―――――――

I can't decide which type of mattress to buy.

I might have to sleep on it.

Making puns about golf is the worst kind of foreplay.

If mimes attended Fight Club, based on the rule of double negatives, would that mean that they WOULD be allowed to talk about it?

What do you call a red-headed baker?

A ginger bread man!

Why are Sherlock Holmes' taxes so low?

He's a master of deduction.

Is this pool safe for diving?

It deep ends.

_____

Did you hear Dracula passed out at
midnight on New Year's Eve?

There was a count down.

I am proud to announce I have completed the very first item on my bucket list.

I have acquired the bucket.

Did you know if you take a blue whale and lay it lengthwise across a football field...

They'll have no choice but to cancel the game.

I asked the waiter if I could get 48 pancakes on a single plate.

He said he wasn't sure, that's a pretty tall order.

Before social media, you could just completely forget someone existed. Good times.

If you spell the word "drawer" backwards, you will get a reward.

_____

Despite the existence of doors, Santa actually prefers going down the chimney.

It soots him.

Just registered for the Global Fruit Preserves Association annual conference.

The agenda is jam packed.

What do you get when you cross a bison with a duck?

Buffalo bill.

This year, I'll be fulfilling my dream of opening my own independent shoe store.

I'll be the sole proprietor.

———

Would it kill the makers of avocados to put a different toy inside? I have like 50 wooden balls already.

Just boarded an airplane and got mistaken for the pilot.

Guess I'm just gonna wing it.

———————

Never throw false teeth at your vehicle. You might denture car.

What do you do if you see a fireman?

Put it out, man.

Never discuss infinity with a mathematician, they can go on about it forever.

Doctor: Describe your average night.

Me: They wear suits of armour.

Doctor: No, I mean at bedtime.

Me: They probably take it off.

What do you call a potato wearing glasses?

A spec-tater!

How many wizards does it take to change a light bulb?

Depends on what you want to change it into.

Why did the candle quit his job?

He was burned out.

Fear of going to the dentist when I was 12: "It's going to hurt!"

Fear of going to the dentist at 47: "He's gonna say I need all new teeth and charge me £30,000!"

———————

I bought a car today and the dealership made me check off – with a pen, on paper – that I am not a robot.

I was so nervous I started sweating coolant.

My partner screamed in pain during labour so I asked, "What's wrong!?"

She replied, "These contractions are going to kill me!!"

"I am sorry, honey," I replied. "What is wrong?"

Procrastination is a dish best served eventually.

I lost an electron. You really have to keep an ion them!

You can't ever trust the king of the jungle.

He's always lion.

A search engine marketing expert walks into a bar, bars, bars near me, pub, tavern, public house, Irish pub, drinks, beer, alcohol place, drinking spot, place for beer, beer now.

———————

Programmers generally don't like nature. Too many bugs.

When astronauts get sick, do they feel over the weather?

_____

Did you know that Albert Einstein was also a talented rapper?

Though you might know him better by his stage name, M.C. Squared.

What do you call a mute owl?

Anything you like, it doesn't give a hoot.

I used to just crastinate but I got so good I went pro.

There are two kinds of people in this world: those who can extrapolate from incomplete data.

How many clickbait articles does it take to change a light bulb?

The answer will shock you!

Very disappointed to find out that the universal remote control I bought does not control the universe.

Not even remotely.

Quit my job at the chemical factory.

It was a toxic work environment.
You should have seen their reaction.
Total meltdown.

———

I told a joke about fractions at work the other day.

Co-workers' opinions were divided.

What do you call it when an undercover pastor leads a short prayer?

A blessing in disguise.

Does cost of living go on sale for Black Friday?

Asking for myself.

The police came out to warn me that the frozen pond I was fishing on was rapidly melting.

I'm not in trouble, but I am walking on thin ice.

———————

If womb is pronounced as "woom" and tomb is pronounced as "toom"…

Then it's only fair that bomb should go "boom".

I know how it will all end for me.

One of my kids will unplug my life support to charge their iPad.

———

What do you call a dying airport computer?

A terminal terminal terminal.

Everyone says that I tend to use outdated technology.

But they're just ignoring the fax.

A guy walks into a bar and sustains a mild concussion.

Woke up this morning to find my stocking drenched with orange soda.

I must've gotten a visit from Fanta Claus.

Why did the belt get arrested?

He held up a pair of pants.

A dentist married a manicurist but they fought tooth and nail.

———————

Teaching children about fungus is one way to mould young minds.

You should never tell someone you love them on January 1st.

It's only the first date!

———————

What did the veggies say at the garden party?

Lettuce turnip the beet.

Did you hear about the promo they're running at the pet store?

Buy one dog, get one flea.

———

Someone once asked me if I knew what the ninth letter of the alphabet was.

It was a complete guess, but I was right.

I wasn't going to visit my family this December, but they promised to make me Eggs Benedict.

So I'm going home for the Hollandaise.

I like my water like I like my emotions.

Bottled up.

What do you call a frequent midnight snacker?

An insom-nom-nom-niac.

Spilled a bunch of crumbs while eating over my keyboard.

But it's all under Ctrl now.

Have you ever had to charge a battery?

It's revolting.

_____

Maturing in marriage is learning to compromise.

My partner wanted Christmas trees in every room in the house and I thought that was too much so we compromised and now there are Christmas trees in every room in the house.

I'm going on a camping trip but I'm not happy with my travel insurance.

Apparently, if my tent blows away during the night I'll no longer be covered.

You know, I used to confuse *Star Wars* and *Star Trek*.

It was a Wookie mistake.

How do the reindeer always know when Santa is near?

They can sense his presents.

If you think time travel is a hassle now, just wait until yesterday.

I found this great place online to order quality sausage.

I'll send you a link.

———

I can't stand it when people call me a hypochondriac.

It makes me sick.

My brother was a lion tamer. When he went bankrupt they took almost everything.

But at least he still has his pride.

_____

I have a scary joke about maths... but I'm 2^2 to say it.

My last apartment only had four-foot high ceilings.

I couldn't stand living there.

_____

Why did people panic when a new body of water appeared?

It was an emergent sea.

I heard a large oil company is going to start making gasoline from insect urine.

I think it's BP.

———

Having a colonoscopy wasn't the most fun I ever had, but it was definitely up there.

My therapist told me I can't identify my own emotions.

I'm not sure how I feel about that.

———————

Where do mansplainers get their water?

From a well, actually.

Why did the orange stop rolling down the hill?

It ran out of juice.

_____

I lost my job as a psychic.

Didn't see that coming!

What kind of lotion does a bullfighter use?

Olay!

_____

What do you call a happy cowboy?

A jolly rancher.

I can't think of any more boat puns.

Canoe?

_____

I used to get heartburn whenever I ate
birthday cake.

Then the doctor suggested I take the
candles off first.

What do ducks like on their tacos?

Quackamole!

———————

**The worst part about being a cab driver
is all the people talking behind
your back.**

I love going outdoors. It's much safer
than going out windows.

Ladies, if your partner asks for matador
equipment for Christmas...
it's a big red flag.

I somehow managed to make it through high school maths while only being able to remember even numbers!

What are the odds?

_____

My partner said one of the tyres on his car needed more pressure.

So I told it if I don't see any improvement in its sales numbers this quarter, it's fired.

My cabinet installer was arrested
last week.

He was charged with counter fitting.

———

Why did the Stormtrooper decide to buy
an iPhone?

Because he couldn't find the Droid he
was looking for.

Have you heard of the Christmas alphabet? It's like the regular alphabet except there's Noel.

———

There are 10 types of people in this world.

Those who understand binary and those who don't.

@DadSaysJokes is a community-run dad jokes network on Instagram, Facebook and X (Twitter), with over eight million followers, inspired by the daily jokes of author Kit Chilvers' dad, Andrew.

Every day, followers submit their jokes and the team picks their favourites – or Dad just drops in his own zinger!

Kit, a young social networking influencer, started his career at the tender age of 14, when he created his original platform, Football.Newz. He has since added another nine platforms, including @PubityPets and monster meme page @Pubity, which has over 38 million followers.

Also available:

 @DadSaysJokes

 @Dadsaysjokes

 @DadSaysJokes